This Nature Storybook belongs to:

_____

_____

WALKER BOOKS

Spotted seahorse
(Hippocampus kuda)

Dwarf seahorse
(Hippocampus zosterae)

Short-snouted seahorse
(Hippocampus hippocampus)

Pacific seahorse
(Hippocampus ingens)

Thorny seahorse
(Hippocampus histrix)

Pygmy seahorse
(Hippocampus bargibanti)

**Lemur-tail
seahorse**
(Hippocampus mohnikei)

**Short-headed
seahorse**
(Hippocampus breviceps)

**Barbour's
seahorse**
(Hippocampus barbouri)

**Zebra
seahorse**
(Hippocampus zebra)

**Long-snouted
seahorse**
(Hippocampus guttulatus)

**Great
seahorse**
(Hippocampus kelloggi)

The author, illustrator and publisher would like to thank
Colin Wells of the National Marine Aquarium in Plymouth for
his expert advice and guidance during the preparation of this book.

First published 2006 by Walker Books Ltd
87 Vauxhall Walk, London SE11 5HJ

This edition published 2015

10 9 8 7 6 5 4 3 2

Text © 2006 by Chris Butterworth
Illustrations © 2006 by John Lawrence

The right of Chris Butterworth and John Lawrence to be identified as author
and illustrator respectively of this work has been asserted by them in
accordance with the Copyright, Designs and Patents Act 1988

This book has been typeset in Lawrence and Slimbach

Printed in China

British Library Cataloguing in Publication Data:
a catalogue record for this book is available from the British Library

ISBN 978-1-4063-6702-7

www.walker.co.uk

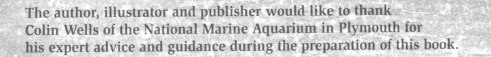

For Margaret
C. B.

For Dominic
J. L.

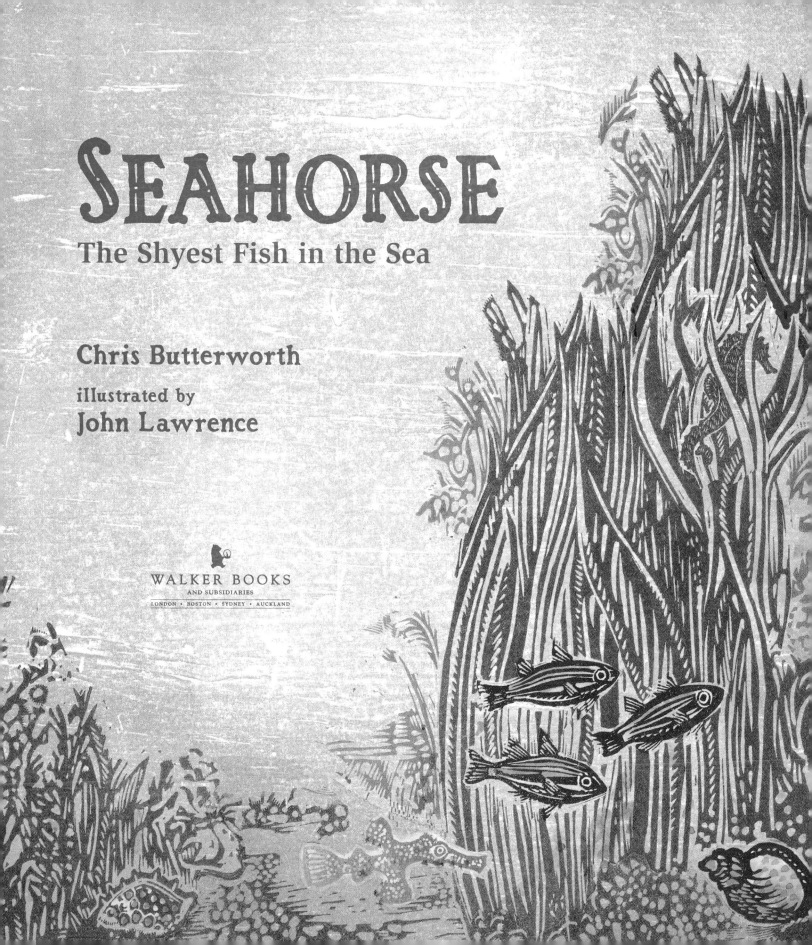

SEAHORSE

The Shyest Fish in the Sea

Chris Butterworth

illustrated by
John Lawrence

WALKER BOOKS
AND SUBSIDIARIES
LONDON · BOSTON · SYDNEY · AUCKLAND

In the warm ocean, among the waving
sea grass meadows, an eye like a small black bead
is watching the fish dart by.
Who does it belong to?

SEAHORSE –
one of the shyest
fish in the sea.

Seahorse has a head
like a horse,
a tail like a monkey and
a pouch like a kangaroo.

This one is a "Barbour's seahorse".
He has tiny prickles down his back like a dragon.
He may not look much like a fish ... but that's what he is.

For a long time, no one was sure what kind of animal the seahorse was.
Its scientific name is "Hippocampus", which means "horse-like sea monster".

Seahorse swims upright. He moves himself through the water with little fins on his head, and a larger one on his back.

He can only
swim slowly,
so if a hungry
snapper cruises by
looking for
a snack, Seahorse
does something
very clever:
he stops still
and changes colour ...   (now you see him ...)

Seahorses have hard bony ridges all down their bodies.
Not many other creatures eat them – probably because they're just too difficult to swallow.

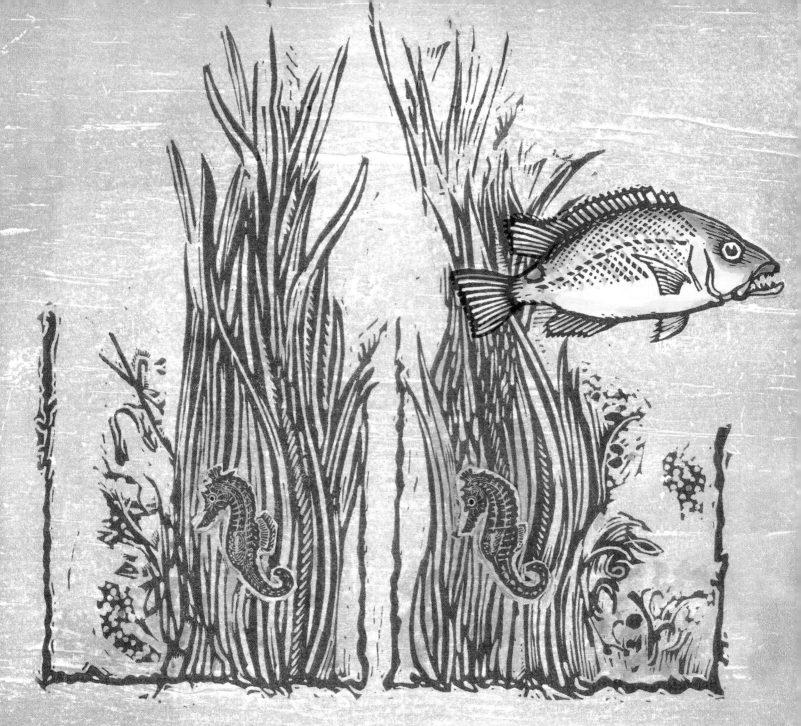

until he's almost invisible   **(now you don't!).**

The way seahorses change the colour of their skin to blend in with
their surroundings is called "camouflage".

Every day at sunrise,
Seahorse swims slowly off
to meet his mate.

They twist their tails together and twirl gently round,
changing colour until they match.

Seahorses are faithful to one mate and often pair up for life.

Today Seahorse's mate
is full of ripe eggs.

The two of them dance till sunset,
and then she puts her eggs into his pouch.

Barbour's seahorses mate every few weeks in the breeding season.
Only male seahorses have a pouch. Only female seahorses can grow eggs.

Seahorse sways about
to get the eggs settled in,
then seals his pouch
tight shut.

Seahorses are the
only male fish to get
"pregnant" like this,
growing their young
inside their
own bodies.

Safe inside, the dots in the eggs
begin to grow into baby
seahorses. They break out
of their eggs and keep on growing,
every one with a head like
a tiny horse and a tail like
a tiny monkey.

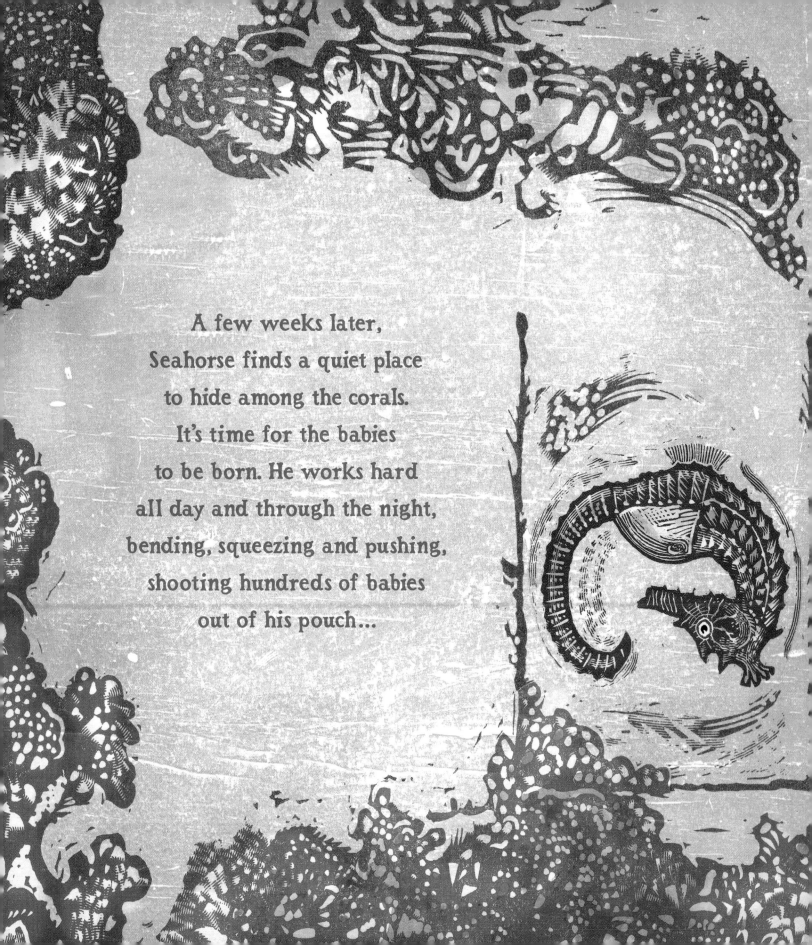

A few weeks later,
Seahorse finds a quiet place
to hide among the corals.
It's time for the babies
to be born. He works hard
all day and through the night,
bending, squeezing and pushing,
shooting hundreds of babies
out of his pouch...

Barbour's seahorses can have two to three hundred babies at one time.

They swirl round him
in the water like smoke.

One or two of the babies hang on to Dad's nose for a bit
(it's the first and biggest thing they've seen),

Each tiny new seahorse is a perfect copy of its parents and is ready for life on its own as soon as it's born.

but when they let go ... they are so tiny and light that
the current soon floats them away.

This new seahorse
is only as long
as your eyelash,
but she can find her
own food straight away.
Her eyes move separately
from each other
(one can peer up while
the other looks down)
so she can spot
food coming from
any direction.

Seahorses live on "plankton" – tiny creatures
that float along with the current.

With one quick slurp
she sucks her catch
into the end
of her snout and
swallows it whole –
seahorses don't have teeth.

To drop lower in the water, seahorses tuck in their necks and roll up their tails.

To rise higher, they uncurl themselves till they are almost as straight as pencils.

When she is big enough, Seahorse curls up her tail and sinks down to the sea bed.

Seahorses cannot live where the currents are very strong. They would be swept away.

Here she is safer. Her camouflage protects her,
and if a storm scoops the sea into huge waves
or passing boats send currents sweeping by,
there are plenty of things to hang on to.

Seahorses have "prehensile" tails, which means
they can grasp things tightly with them.

When she is bigger still, Seahorse picks one patch of reef as her home.

She wraps her tail round a coral branch. This is her "holdfast" ... wherever she goes, she'll keep coming back to this holdfast.

Male Barbour's seahorses only range over a few square metres. The females' range is twice as big, or even bigger.

In a few months
this little seahorse
will be ready to mate.
She'll spend the rest of her
life on the reef, watching
for food, meeting
her mate and
trying to stay
almost invisible...

Barbour's seahorses can mate
by six months and are fully
grown at about a year.

Who's that
peering from the coral?

Shhhh, she's a seahorse.

Index

Look up the pages to find out about all these seahorse things.
Don't forget to look at both kinds of word – **this kind** and this kind.

About the author

Chris Butterworth loves the sea and the amazing things that live in it. "A seahorse looks as magical as a mermaid," she says, "but while mermaids are made up, seahorses really exist. We need to know as much as we can about them, so we can protect them better. Otherwise, one day seahorses might join the mermaids and only exist in stories."

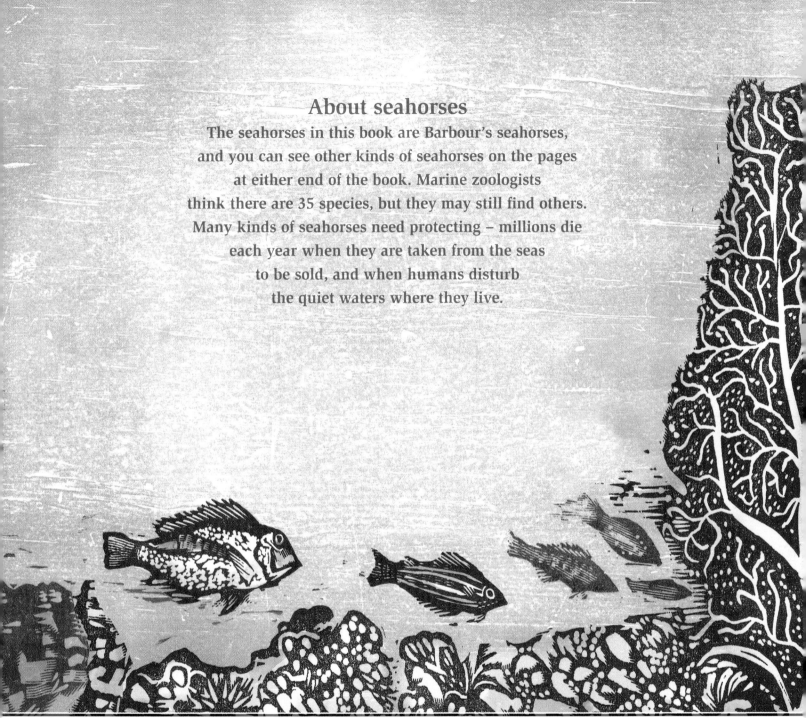

About seahorses

The seahorses in this book are Barbour's seahorses,
and you can see other kinds of seahorses on the pages
at either end of the book. Marine zoologists
think there are 35 species, but they may still find others.
Many kinds of seahorses need protecting – millions die
each year when they are taken from the seas
to be sold, and when humans disturb
the quiet waters where they live.

About the illustrator

John Lawrence was born by the sea and has always loved swimming and pottering along
the shore. "I never met any seahorses," he says, "so this book has given me the
opportunity I missed. They are really exciting to draw and I have tried to imagine how
it must be to live under the water like them."

Spotted seahorse
(Hippocampus kuda)

Dwarf seahorse
(Hippocampus zosterae)

Short-snouted seahorse
(Hippocampus hippocampus)

Pacific seahorse
(Hippocampus ingens)

Thorny seahorse
(Hippocampus histrix)

Pygmy seahorse
(Hippocampus bargibanti)

Lemur-tail seahorse
(Hippocampus mohnikei)

Short-headed seahorse
(Hippocampus breviceps)

Barbour's seahorse
(Hippocampus barbouri)

Zebra seahorse
(Hippocampus zebra)

Long-snouted seahorse
(Hippocampus guttulatus)

Great seahorse
(Hippocampus kelloggi)

Note to Parents

Sharing books with children is one of the best ways to help them learn. And it's one of the best ways they learn to read, too.

Nature Storybooks are beautifully illustrated, award-winning information picture books whose focus on animals has a strong appeal for children. They can be read as stories, revisited and enjoyed again and again, inviting children to become excited about a subject, to think and discover, and to want to find out more.

Each book is an adventure into the real world that broadens children's experience and develops their curiosity and understanding – and that's the best kind of learning there is.

Note to Teachers

Nature Storybooks provide memorable reading experiences for children in Key Stages 1 and 2 (Years 1–4), and also offer many learning opportunities for exploring a topic through words and pictures.

By working with the stories, either individually or together, children can respond to the animal world through a variety of activities, including drawing and painting, role play, talking and writing.

The books provide a rich starting-point for further research and for developing children's knowledge of information genres.

Nature Storybooks support the literacy curriculum in a variety of ways, providing:

- a focus for a whole class topic
- high-quality texts for guided reading
- a resource for the class read-aloud programme
- information texts for the class and school library for developing children's individual reading interests

Find more information on how to use Nature Storybooks in the classroom at
www.walker.co.uk/naturestorybooks
Nature Storybooks support KS 1–2 English and KS 1–2 Science